Josh and the big boys

"I am going to play

on the slide,"

said Josh.

"Oh, no!

The big boys

are on the slide."

"I am going to play
on the swings,"
said Josh.

"Oh, no!

The big boys

are on the swings."

"I am going to play
on the monkey bars,"
said Josh.

"Oh, no!

The big boys

are on the monkey bars."

"Come and play

on the monkey bars,"

said a big boy.

"Look at me!" said Josh.

"I am on the monkey bars, too."